A Translation Of Shadows

a play by Stan's Cafe

ISBN 978-1-913185-18-3

Published by Stan's Cafe
Birmingham, UK
2020

www.stanscafe.co.uk

A Translation Of Shadows © Stan's Cafe 2015
Production photos © Graeme Braidwood 2015
Stills and other photos © Stan's Cafe 2015

Publication © Stan's Cafe 2020

Contents:

A Translation Of Shadows	1
Bonus Material	
Original programme note	52
Theatre credits	53
Outline for the film *Shadows*	54
Woman Of Tokyo (1933) by Yasujirō Ozu – Benshi Script	60
Making *A Translation Of Shadows*	69

A Translation Of Shadows

Benshi: Welcome everyone... good evening.

It's lovely to see lots of familiar faces. Those of you who follow me from place to place or come back, time after time, thank you. I also see some new faces. Some beautiful new faces, hello indeed, thank you for bringing that face to this place.

Now, for those of you who are new, this is how tonight works. Behind me is this screen and onto this screen will be projected a film.

For those of you new to films, films are a sequence of moving pictures that together tell a story. Films are also illusions, Ladies and Gentlemen, the stories they tell have rarely happened and the pictures themselves do not really move. The film is built from a sequence of still photographs projected in such rapid succession that our minds endow them with the quality of movement and translate them into stories.

"How were these still photographs created?" the inquisitive amongst you will ask. Well, a long time ago, in a place far away, light struck every object you are about to see in this film, Ladies and Gentlemen, and a portion of that light bounced from each of these objects into a lens. This lens focused that reflected light into the body of a camera where, split into red, green and blue components, this light, in all its softness and intensity, was converted into electrical impulses and a stream of blinking ones and zeros. And so, for your wonderment this evening, we have the Sanyo PLV XM100L, you may see its lens poking cheekily from the balcony above you. This 'beamer' as our German cousins would have it, will generate a light source and pass it

through a matrix of rotating mirrors, one mirror per pixel, each directing light to or from both the lens and a colour wheel. This miracle machine, Ladies and Gentlemen, will translate that stream of zeros and ones back into the beautiful images you are to see on this screen tonight.

Now I appreciate a few of you may not have come for a lecture on film technology, you have come for drama, for romance, for mystery, for intrigue, for horror and for laughter. Well, you have come to the right place, for this, is a cinema.

Now do not worry Ladies and Gentlemen, I will be here throughout to translate for you. I could have been up there... but I have chosen to stay down here with you, the real people. I am the Benshi. There are many people in this film, indeed many makers of this film and many of you in the audience, but there is only one Benshi and that Benshi is me and I am here to guide you through the film, helping you to read and understand it, while adding my own inimitable colour.

Talking of colour, you may have noticed my outfit, it may give you a clue as to tonight's film and where it will transport us to... that's right madam... to Japan.

Japan... 7000 islands, volcanoes, earthquakes, cherry blossom, technology, bright lights, 130 million people each with their own story. We all have a story of course, something that sets us apart, some of us have more stories than others of course, we have seen more, done more, felt more, we have taken things just that little bit further...

Now we could, of course, just listen to me all night, I know I could, but we have a film to share, a film called... Shadows.

[Theme tune music and move to lectern]

> And now, before Ben starts up the projector, let us pause and savour this moment. Let's treasure this time when everything is quiet and still, the time before the screen reveals its secrets, when anything is possible and anything might happen…

[Film Starts with credits]

Card 1: Shadows
Card 2: These are the names of actors. The Japanese read from top to bottom right to left.
Card 3: Etc.
Opening shot: Right! The streets of Tokyo.
> Tokyo, as I'm sure you all know, is one of the most populous cities in the world with over 13 million people… a city teeming with life…
> although you wouldn't think so to look at this particular shot. The cars and trains, everything is familiar and yet somehow different.

Apartment exterior: Exterior. High rise buildings, offices, apartments and in one of these small apartments…

Interior: Interior. A girl, a young woman, straightens her hair in one of three mirrors, one perhaps not enough to reflect all her beauty. One woman. One day. Today?

Putting on make up: We humans have been making ourselves up for thousands of years, with henna, red ochre, bees wax, olive oil, rice powder, kohl, white lead, arsenic, decorating ourselves for acts of war, acts of deception, acts of worship and acts of love. We paint our faces and our bodies, we make them darker, we make them paler, we add colour, we disguise fatigue, we mask our imperfections, we cover up our spots, we give ourselves spots. We transform ourselves to make ourselves more attractive, our skin softer, our lips more kissable. Imagine kissing those lips.
> It is as if she has no idea we are watching her. As if she thinks she is alone.

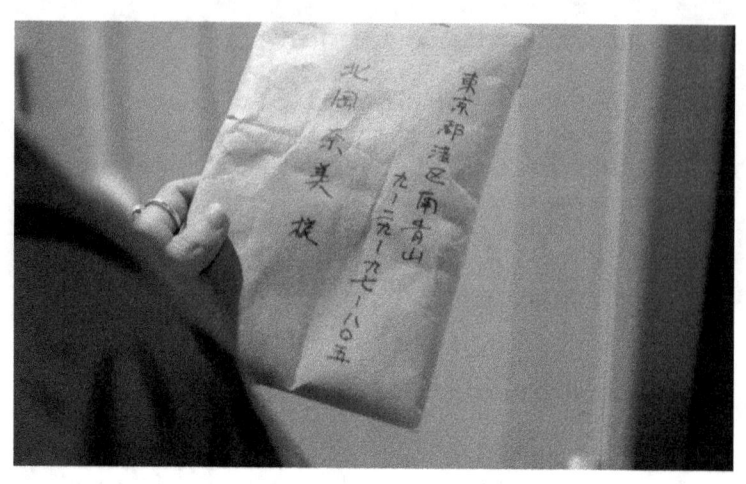

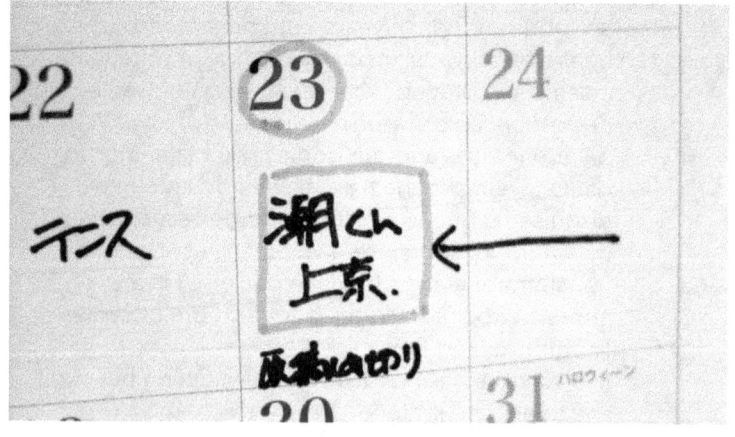

There's that smile, the smile that the Japanese loved
and which made her a star.

Picks up headphones: Big close up.
Photograph: Her mother.
Down on mailbox: The door to her apartment.
As she leaves she checks her mailbox. She
recognises the hand writing. She checks the franking
mark. She is pleased with it. She will open it later.
Keep an eye on that envelope ladies and
gentlemen, we don't see anything in a film that isn't
important, in that respect film is so much more
straightforward than real life.

Exterior: Here, Ladies and Gentlemen, this is an important
point to note, we are now out on the streets with the
woman but we didn't see her walk down the stairs or
out from her apartment building. We are expected
to fill in this gap. If the film maker cannot rely on us
to do this work for ourselves then he must show us
everything, in which case this film would be 32 hours
long and nobody wants to watch a 32 hour long film
do they Ladies and Gentlemen?

Now, we saw a calendar earlier, on her wall, with a
date marked in red. Do you remember? Is this that
day? We must presume it is; no one makes a film
about an ordinary day. So what makes it special?
How will this story unfold? At this point we can only
speculate, but we know stories and how they work...

The ending has already been written of course and
filmed. We could skip to the final reel, miss out the
exposition, cut to the climax and drop the director's
quirks, like the over indulgent shot of the train we
saw earlier... but perhaps you enjoyed that Madam?
You took pleasure simply in the visual wonder of that
moment? We don't all need pure narrative to keep
us engaged do we Sir? We can see beauty

everywhere we choose to see beauty, even in the traffic-choked streets of Tokyo.

Couple: We could follow any of these people. What about this couple? Do they perform this little dance together every morning? If we are interested in them we are out of luck, the film is interested in her, my… our girl, as she makes her way down into Gaiemmae Station on the Ginza subway line. Look how petite she is, petite but confident. She looks at no-one you see… eyes fixed on her device… oblivious … except there. You see a little glance to her left? I think that's a mistake. In life something may attract us or distract us and we may glance at it and it means nothing, but here, in this film? As an audience we are alert to the work we must do, we try to attach meaning to this glance and there is none, now it is we who are distracted. If this were my film, I would have reshot that moment.

On Train: Now, here she is on the train and remember that envelope Ladies and Gentlemen? I told you we would see it again. Now at last we shall see what's inside it. Can you guess? It's a padded envelope so… It is a shell and on the shell is written a message. It says 'See you soon'. Who will she see? Look for that Mana Fuji smile, Ladies and Gentlemen. Anyone who can make her smile like that must surely be someone special.

Crossing Gates: *[Reading from a card]* Slender arms descend
Hazard lights keep flashing stop
Yet the breeze blows on

They Fish: This timeless landscape that the earth spewed up is theirs. The fishermen, time is their currency, they drift with its ebb and flow, waiting patiently for their catch. They are not hunters. They are harvesters. This is a moment, lifted out of time by those

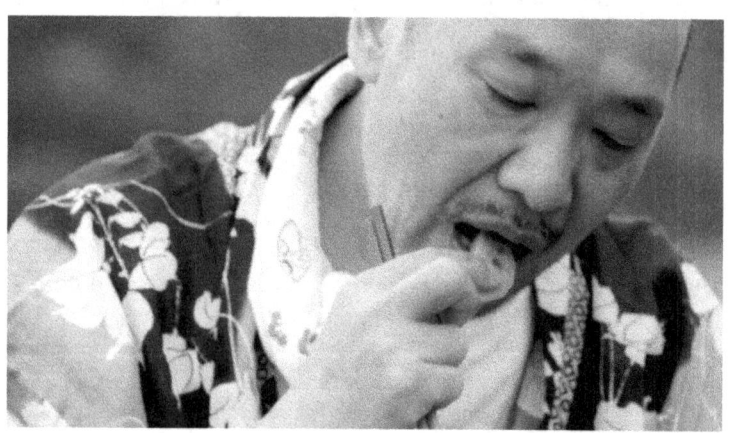

watching. The film crew waited days for this shot, the director spent hours looking at the skies waiting for this cloud cover, this calm, this light, this moment.

They decide to stop for the day. There will be another.

Boy: "Nothing today" the son says.
Father: "No, maybe you will have more luck in Tokyo".
"She will be waiting for me".
"She is a fine catch".
The father is surefooted, the son less so.
The farther is patient, the son less so.
Now we have these first two scenes linked. Surely this young fisherman must be the person who sent the shell to the girl.

They eat:
Father: A bento box. That's like a lunch box.
"I don't want you to go".
"Father, I must".
"I will miss you".
"I will return. I will return with her. I will be gone just one day".
"Tokyo will swallow you, you will drown".
"I can swim. I belong here father, I will return"

Lotus Root: This is lotus root.

Long shot: What if she doesn't wish to return with you, sonny?

Crab: This is interesting – the crab – you might think it refers to astrology, any Cancerians in tonight? But no, in Japan they look more to blood type as an indicator of personality than they do the stars. Perhaps we are meant to think of how crabs must shed their outer shell in order to grow. Perhaps we are to witness a rebirth.

Boy's Room: Interior. We are in their simple home.
His room.
Now watch carefully, there are many clues here, it's almost like a crime scene. A simple room but clean,

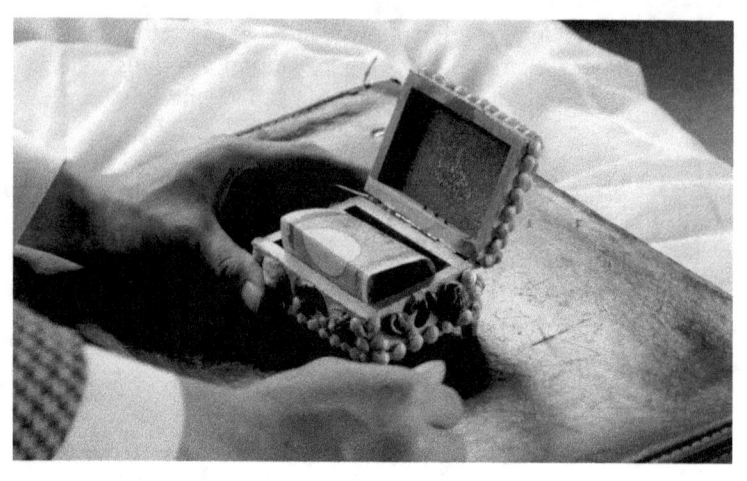

lots of postcards (Tokyo), a suit – well a jacket and trousers (dressing up); a tatty suitcase (a journey is implied); a box covered in shells (shells, Ladies and Gentlemen) and money, Yen – the Japanese currency – all his savings going into that wallet. It looks like a lot but they don't have pounds and pence, it's all Yen. Note, no credit card, no ID (a self-contained man). One particular postcard. A date circled on a calendar. All the information we require.

Boy leaves home: This is Kakamoto Eshi in his first film. It is difficult for many Japanese to reconcile this image with his later roles but his background was not far from that of the simple young man he plays here. In the background: octopus traps, they float in but cannot swim out.

Catching the Train.
Establishing shot: *[Reading from a card]* Aluminium Dreams. Airbrush canvas dalmatian sky.
Coach Pulls off: A coach thrown sunbeam.
He walks across frame: So, the journey to the start of the journey has finished.
He is at the train station.
From here it is possible to go anywhere
to a thriller, a kidnapping, a romance, a horror.
He can go anywhere, but first he must buy a ticket.
As we all must buy a ticket.
Security Mirror: And yet it is not that easy, you must decide where it is you wish to go. The city, yes the city, but the city has many stations and each station is the start of so many stories: Shinigawa, Shimbashi, Kyobashi, Ikebukuro, Shinjuku.
He starts to buy ticket: Return tickets are so expensive.
"Tokyo will swallow you, you will drown".
"I belong here father, I will return".
Wallet: A return will cost him almost everything, dare he leave nothing to chance?
The Yen to go. The Yen to return.

Everything rides on the difference.
Already he feels his promise slipping away.
He buys a single ticket. He will try to save his money for the return.

Through security barrier: His fate is sealed.

Walking above platforms:

POV walking above platform: Point-of-View shot (hand held) "Be strong Kiguchi San, all will be well. You will be fine. I will be fine. Platform 2, 15:57, plenty of time. Shibuya Station, Tamagawa Entrance 'I will be waiting for you just past the ticket barriers'".

He walks down stairs: He is walking away from his loving father, but what of his mother? Because she is absent should we assume she is dead? "The motherless boy travels to the city to find a woman, to rescue a woman, to replace a woman, to find his mother, to kiss the girl". The storytellers are pulling levers in our minds that we do not recognise as levers, Ladies and Gentlemen. Trust me to keep you safe, hold my hand Ladies and Gentleman as we board the train. The last carriage of the long train at

He walks to end of train: the very far end of the local stopping line to Tokyo. Step aboard with me ladies and gentlemen.

He is sat on train: The Kubuki acting technique: show excitement, anticipation, anxiety, confusion, 'let's go'!

The train pulls off: The maglev train uses repulsion. The train does not touch its rails. Everything is easy because everything is afloat. There is no friction.
This is not a maglev train.

Train into distance: Things touch, they judder, they shake, they squeal.

He snoozes on train: He is drowsy (he was fishing at dawn). We are about to see a special cameo appearance from, Tokuko Nagai Takagi, the first woman to act in a Japanese film. Before her, only men could be women on film.

Handles dangle: This train is a conduit between worlds,

travelling to the future, he is enveloped.

Him asleep: "I dream. I dream I am awake another layer down. My ticket is a post card. Which way is north? How fast are we travelling? How far have we gone? When will be we there? I am lost. Everyone around me is dreaming, we meet in our dreams, we drift in the floating world, we drift."

Working Late.

Opening shot: You are on your own then.
   No one can see you – except us, we are watching yes,

Second shot: we can see you, yes.

Typing on computer: You are so busy, so smart, so important.

Shot of Neck: Your skin is so smooth, your neck.

Look up at clock: You are preparing for me, to meet me. That smile was for me, you are thinking of me as you're working.

Reaches for water: No, I don't like the water bit NO!
   [Hand up to rewind and divert the film]

Shot of Neck: Your skin is so smooth, your neck.

Look up at clock: You are preparing for me, to meet me. That smile was for me, you are thinking of me even as you work. Each task brings me nearer.

Lever arch file:

Light off: No, you're not leaving. You're not ready to go. You're not finished, there's more.
   [Hand up to divert the film]

Mysterious papers arrive: There's more to do!

She looks around: *[Laughs]*
   You can't see me but I am watching. I can see you.

She looks down: That's it. There's more to do.

Turning pages: There are more facts, more figures, more columns to add. You like to be in control. You don't like to leave things unfinished, so you can't leave.

Clock on wall: We must spend more time together. That delicate necklace, that light blouse. The director did not frame you as I would. He did not make the best of you.

                Nearly finished? Yes, you're tired, it's been a long
                day. Are you stressed because you think you may
                miss your kooky boyfriend from the sticks? Shame.
Walking across room: Now you think you're done.
Flicks lights off: You think you're escaping.
Phone on table: *[Telephone rings]*
She picks up: Moshi Moshi. You must hurry, you're late.
She hangs up: Nice speaking with you.

On the Train.
Mouth open reflection: "*[Gasp]* now we are close, you are
                rushing, rattling, flickering into view.
Glide: Now we glide.
            Thirteen million and one spots of light.
            In my dream I am dazzled.
Blur focus: I try and focus.
            I am still dreaming of you.
            We are closer with every passing moment.

            We will come together and when we touch
            we will hold to keep from drifting apart.
            We will kiss.
            Our lights will coalesce
            and soon it will be daylight.

            Time is slowing.
            Parallel lives are catching ours and we are catching
            them.
            "Nami, we must cling to who we wish to be!"
            That's what I'd be thinking, he's probably got a head
            full of shrimp.

Looped corridor sequence: *[Hand up until he lets her go]*
            Wait! Time and space don't always behave as they
            should do they? We've got all the time there is.
            We can loop this forever.

Final mirror shot: Okay. Go. Run!

Rush to the Station.
Neon Light:
Train Pulls in: Haemoglobin. Corpuscular. Platelets floating.
> City pulse in the alveoli, deep carbon exchange, aorta flow.

Him off Train: Ventricle contracting, breath in, breath out, breath in, breath out. Deep breaths. Pulmonary station.
> 13 million people processed, proceed.

Up Escalator: Heads, brains, thoughts, sliding by, unheard voices, lost stories.

Her out of office:

Her getting in taxi: "Shibuya Station, fast!"

Shot of taxi driver:

Looks at watch: "Quick as you can!"
> Watch the watch, everything you see in film is important.
>
> She was just ninteen when she shot to fame. A shop assistant at a high end boutique. An agent friend. A rapid ascent. A natural charm and face for the camera. For a long time she never looked back

Windscreen & glove: "Who is this guy? Does he know where he's going?
> Is this the route?
> Why is he slowing?"

He arrives: "Shibuya Station. Tamagawa Entrance, I will be waiting".
> He moved to Tokyo to become an actor. He was talented but impulsive and wild, wrong for so many roles.

Stands and watches: *[Reading from a card]* The modest heron.
> Standing by, too shy to strike.
> Killing time, not yet.

Gloves and looking round: "What crazy route is this? I don't recognise any of this!"

Stops & Bus: Deep metropolis currents, krill, tuna, sharks. The dragnet.

He takes p/c out: "I will be waiting", "I will be waiting unless you have the wrong time, or the wrong place..."

Japanese trains are never late "I will be waiting, unless something goes wrong", "unless my boyfriend has me tied up and won't let me go", "unless I never liked you at all".

Her in taxi: "Unless... unless I'm in a taxi with a killer..."

Taxi moves: Her agent chose her roles for her, mostly romantic comedies. Jump to the fast lane and stay there. Eventually she came to feel trapped in her screen persona and longed for more assertive roles.

Taxi pulls up: "Hold on, what are you doing?"

Talking to driver: "Why are you stopping? What's going on?"

Driver to her: "We've run out of petrol, this is as far as we go".

Her to driver: "What kind of taxi driver are you to run out of petrol? That's ridiculous! What am I supposed to do now? I'm late already? I've got someone waiting!"

Driver to her: "That's not my problem. Pay me 100 yen and find your own way. We're close now, you can run from here".

Her, interior: "No way! Tell me this is a joke right! Where's the camera? This is a joke right!"

Driver to her: "Hey what the..."

Her out of cab: *[Wearing gloves]* In Tokyo all taxi drivers wear white gloves, Ladies and Gentlemen, but none ever run out of petrol.

Big bridge: *[Running breaths]* Run Nami, run!

Street level: Run Nami, run!

Him at station: He did more waiting than acting. He was older than her when they met. She was more experienced than him.

Puts s/case down: You don't see anything in a film that is not important. He was arrogant, so was she by now. They shared the arrogance of beauty.

He sits: Hash tag: running through the streets of Tokyo to be with him.

She runs: Have you ever truly let someone down Ladies and Gentlemen? Got your priorities wrong and not been there for someone when they needed you, Ladies and Gentlemen? This is what we are witnessing now, and I must tell you, it is ugly.

Waiting on curb: On your marks, get set, go!
She starts running: Run, run or he will be gone!
> You try to do too much. You promise too much and are over optimistic. The uncomfortable truth is you did not value this person enough to be there for them when they needed you.

Shoes: You were not prepared to make the sacrifice for them. Excuses count for nothing. They are abandoned. Does this sound familiar, Ladies and Gentlemen?

Shot from behind: All these things standing in your way now would not been here now if you had started then. You are late.

Him sat at station: Hash tag: you've got no number, no mobile, just enough money to get you home. Her address and everything you own is in that suitcase. They met in a cafe when he was close to destitute. She persuaded him to audition. In his biography he says this was when they first kissed. This audition was his big break. He had nothing to lose. He got the part.

P/C out again: Watch the suitcase. Everything he owns is in there.
He stands: Watch the man in black, watch him, watch him!
Ryuhi steels s/case: Too late! *[Brandishes suitcase]* Tokyo the safest big city in the world.
She runs down stairs: Run Nami, run! You can still make it if you run Nami, run Nami.
Ryuhi stops her: Excuse me, do you have the time?
> Surely you must? I can't let you go.
> Just two more seconds. Okay?

Bag is gone: Undershot. Handheld
Ryuhi into shot: "I've got to ask you to leave sir, you can't wait here".
> "But my bag's been stolen, I'm waiting for someone!"

Long shot: "You have to go. We can't have vagrants at the station".

Wallet out: "I'm not a vagrant! I have money"
Close him speaking: "Where are you staying tonight?"
>"In Roppongi, I have a card, you've got to listen to me!" He has forgotten the address.
>"You're not welcome here".

Shot of his back: "Piss off!"
She runs into shot: Too late, too late, too late. He's been washed from the rock by the current, or maybe he was never here. You wouldn't recognise him anyway would you, a man you last saw fourteen years ago, when he was a boy, when he was ten?
She looks round: Where is he now? He's been lost without tra…oh. He's been swallowed by the shoals.
She picks up card: 13 million people.
Long shot: A plot point has been introduced. Where do we go from here?

Through the Night.

Him on the Crossing: Now the fisherman has his wish, to be a hunter and not a harvester.
POV on Crossing: This sequence is one of the most expensive in movie history, thousands of extras choreographed by the world's greatest choreographers, rehearsed for months on an exact replica of Tokyo's Shibuya crossing, until we have this perfect play of space, bodies and trajectories and everyone you see knows to the millimetre what path they must tread.
Him on crossing: And the remarkable thing, Ladies and Gentlemen, is that, as a result of all that rehearsal, when they came to shoot this sequence, they captured it all in a single take.
Neon signs: But what we cannot tell from the records, or get any of the thousands of supporting artists to divulge, is whether this sequence was filmed on the actual Shibuya crossing or on that simulacra, built six hundred miles away in Nemuro.

Her in Bathroom L/S: There you are. Come closer.
Close Up: Toes

	Thumb in your instep
	Ankle.
	Those poor feet, they need comfort
Face:	You need comfort.
	You should be in the shower.
	I'd have shot this differently.
	Don't think about him. He's gone.
	Long shot.

Long shot: He didn't wait for you.
Rub… him… out of your mind.
Close up.
Face: Before it's too late.
Street: These are the streets of Tokyo. You can't really do this route he's walking, they're mixing the city up; they did that in her race to the station but I didn't want to spoil the illusion for you.
Him Walking: It's difficult to say what Kakamoto is thinking here: Genuine awe? Wonder? Fear? Or something more technical, about his muscles, angles and pace. Maybe he's thinking about her, the character or actress.
POV: He loved motorbikes, the faster the better. The rush kept him alive he said. He bought his first bike with money from this film. When she vanished he fled the city and drove and drove.

Her Eating.

She eats: The rookie detective working through the night, piecing together clues. The young politician wrestling with a dilemma, struggling to do what's right. The teenager comfort eating after a break up. The young mother, up all night nursing a sick child. Her romantic comedies always had this moment and here she is, in this same pose, in her final film.

Him Eating:

He talks to umbrella: How do you find the one person you need to see in a city of thirteen million people? What strategies do you use? How many years would you have to walk the streets? How many street cafes

would you have to eat at?
At Cafe: This is a very important moment. If you have started to drift now would be a good time to focus again.
Long shot: We know how much he has in the wallet. We know how much it will cost him to return home. He will not return home.
Him eating: I like this shot.

Her on Balcony (CU):
Longer:
Closer:
Close: It's late Nami.
 You need to go to bed.
 You have work in the morning.
Him on street:
He starts walking: He is swimming deep now, into the realms of coral and exotic fish; the tiger fish, the clown fish, the blow fish; the rays and the sharks; fish that aren't fish, the Jellyfish and starfish; the vampire squid, the giant spider crab, arrow worms, pyrosoma; strange creatures that never see daylight; a world of bioluminescence.
Shakespeare: He is well out of his depth.
 By the sea he drank beer and smoked pot with his mates to pass the time but now, in this city, with money, mixing with new friends, he was inevitably going to be faced with new temptations. So was she with him. It is difficult to get to the bottom of who introduced whom to the worst of the chemicals that surely destroyed them both for some time.
Into arcade: He had a choice, he chose work and fame and her and everything. They went too deep. Together, they gambled their lives, each urging the other deeper, until the pressure threatened to crush them. And as they tried to surface they lost orientation and balance, nitrogen bubbled in their veins; they hallucinated.
Outside again: The drugs made him paranoid, they gave him different roles, he was both toxic and box office

gold.
That was after this, this is just acting.
Her on the Sofa:
She's dozy: It's been a long day.
> You've been through every emotion, all out of sequence.
>
> And you're still working now, trying to picture him in your mind, out there, lost, confused, scared.

She looks at door: He's not there you know.
> He's probably in a hotel room or in a bar drinking with the crew, with someone else.

Her on sofa: This is where you belong.
> In the city.
>
> He wants you to go back with him. Did you know that?
>
> By the sea you would be a fish out of water, convulsing, gasping on a rock.
>
> He has you frozen in time, endlessly looped, playing on a beach, not even sweethearts.
>
> But you have grown up and are no longer who he imagines.

Him walking: This is a different world. He should have stayed where he was. You shouldn't have encouraged him.

At The Shrine.

Opening & Temple: The Sensoji Temple is the oldest in Japan, it has been on this site for over a thousand years, but none of this is original, it was bombed in the war and rebuilt.

Long Shot: Late at night, tired, he wanders into a corner of a temple to rest. Where do you go when you are desperate Ladies and Gentlemen? Ladies and gentlemen, where would you go for help if you were hundreds of miles from home, in a strange city? What would you do, if you were alone in Tokyo? Have you ever been lost? Have you ever been alone?
> Have you ever been desperate, without friends, in the rain with an empty wallet...

Coins in hand: ...and your last few yen in your hand?
Looks Round: What will he do?
> This, Ladies and Gentlemen, is a plot point; watch carefully.

Puts money down: He takes his last few coins and places them on the Benshi shrine.
> Who better to change your life and turn your luck around than the narrator of your story?

Claps: *[Claps]*
> Will it help? Can you bribe the Gods or is it already too late to edit your story?
>
> Do the Gods exist or are you truly alone?

Coins in pile: *[With coins]*
> Surely it's worth a gamble. What harm can it do?

Bridge and Water.

He Sees the Fish Poster: Towa Sea Food Company Limited.
Him on Bridge Long: *[Reading from a card]*
> The concrete canyon,
> Cradles a moonlit ribbon,
> Path to the ocean.

Him by Lake: Ten takes, late night, everyone frustrated. Their relationship was brief and stormy. They were married briefly. He was suddenly big box office, unfaithful, staggering from one job to the next. Tragically photos emerged of her, maybe from him, unconscious, sprawled on a sofa, make-up streaked across her face.
> The river carries time downstream, change washes over us all.

She Wakes.
City at Dawn: *[Reading from a card]*
    Cold blue light of dawn,
    The calcium city wakes,
    Time snaps back to now.
She is asleep: She is not dead. She couldn't keep herself awake for him. She is dreaming. She is seeing faces, hearing voices. The pictures are so vivid, the voice seems so real, it slowly, gently, softly asks her to "wake up".
She wakes: Now she is awake.
    Her point of View.
POV Balcony:
She looks at watch: Has the time for dreams past?
    "What time is it?"
    Has the time for mysteries past?
    Was last night just a film watched from the sofa on a laptop?
She Stands: *[Trying to control the film]* Don't go to the corner. Don't look on the shelf.
    Point of view.
POV: Hold it. Hold it. Hold…
Shot of her: Don't pick up the shell! Don't look at the shell!
Writing on shell: "Never see you again"
She looks from window: Don't pretend to be worried about him. No, "Never see you again".
She has idea: Don't have an idea. Don't leave. Why isn't this working! Don't go!
Leaves: We lost her. His star continued to rise. She disappeared. He sobered up, but his motorbike eventually hit a wall. She wasn't at the funeral. She never made another film. He made far too many. They should never have met and once met, they should never have kissed.

Fish Market.
Market over river: Establishing shot. Tsukiji Market.
Market interior: Interior. The tuna auction.
She looks:

Rows of frozen Tuna: When a fisherman is lost in the city where does he go? And how does he find his way there?

Tuna out of container:

Her close: This is not her world, it is a gangster world of frozen corpses and she is high and dry...

Longer shot: ...on a bridge, high above the icy flow of commerce.

Closer: Looking down into the pools, through the surface ripples, she tries to catch a glimpse of a life below the surface, a sight of him. Tokyo cannot have drowned him. Surely the Gods of Narrative wouldn't abandon them like this.

POV of Stairs Closer: She takes a deep breath and dives...

Down Stairs: ...and dives.

At Bottom POV: It is cold and hostile in the water.

Long shot of stairs:

POV: She stays under as long as she dare.

Long shot of stairs:

POV: There is no sign of him.

Long shot of stairs: She must return to the surface.

Back at top: Maybe that's it. Maybe she will never see him again.

Her up him down: But of course the Gods of Narrative ordain her logic must work, Ladies and Gentlemen. We know they have a weakness for intuition and poetic justice, just as the Japanese have a weakness for tuna.

We know they must meet, but for now...

He scrubs floor: ...he is the harvester from the country who sought to be a hunter in the city, but now he must scrub vast floors with a minuscule brush.

Exterior establishing:
She sits waiting: She has given up hope. She was so sure and now it seems she was wrong.
Close on her: The wind plays hair across her face, beautiful,
He walks out: but she is in a film where happy endings rule.
He speaks to her: "Hello. Can I help you?"
Down on her: "No, I was looking for someone…"
Close on him: "I think that you've found them, at last".
Close on her: "Yes, it's good to see you. I'm sorry about last night, things got strange".
Mid on him: "That's okay. I'm sorry. I tried waiting for you".
Mid on her: "Never mind, it's okay now, do you want breakfast?"
Mid on him: "I'm sorry, I've got no money, I can't afford it".
She walks off: "Don't worry about that, I'll pay, it's not a problem".
He puts broom down: "I've got my work, but I'm due a break".
Old folk on street: So, Ladies and Gentlemen, another saccharine dénouement looms over another soppy story. But it nearly didn't end like this. How do I know? Remember, I told you, I could have been up there.

Cafe.

[Benshi voices Him. Her voice is dubbed and doesn't match her lips on the screen.]

Him: "I've been waiting a long time for this conversation, do you mind if I ask you some questions?"

Her: "I don't normally allow journalists to interview me whilst I'm filming but you seemed very serious, very professional".

Him: "I wanted to ask – um – are you happy?"

Her: "That's not a very usual question".

Him: "It seems to me, looking at your recent work that you are not".

Her: "You think you can tell that from my films".

Him: "Yes, looking carefully. You're brilliant of course, but it is as if you are frustrated, you want something more challenging, that you could get your teeth

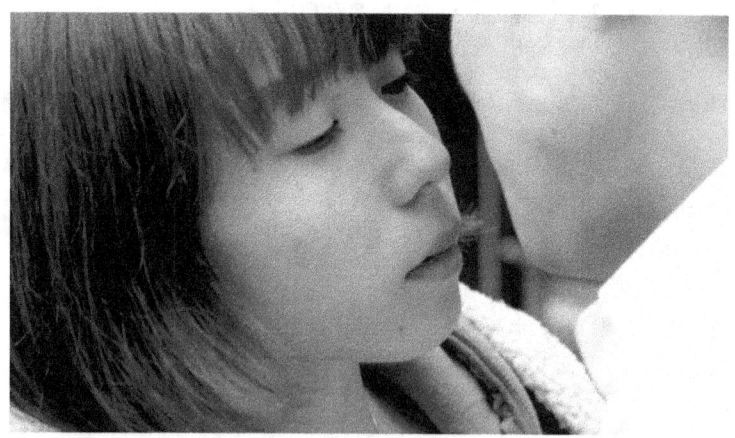

	into. You can do so much better than this film".
Her:	"Yes, that's right. I want something dramatic".
Him:	"I imagine you in a historical epic, as a warrior queen... I've got a script".
Her:	"Something you've written? This really isn't how it works, my agent deals with my scripts and I don't like thinking about one project before I have finished the one I'm working on".
Him:	"I'm sorry".
Her:	"But it sounds intriguing. It's not like anything that I've worked on before. I do want to stretch myself and the idea of a Warrior Queen is interesting, how would it be financed? Is it likely to happen? Do you know who would direct it?"
Him:	"Well, I would direct it. It would be a project we worked on closely together".
Her:	"Well, that sounds wonderful, could we do it? Really?"
Him:	"Sure, I've made lots of art house film, they're highly regarded in the UK. We'd hire a castle and shoot it on location in Scotland".
Her:	"Scotland? That sounds amazing!"
Him:	"It would be spectacular, really beautiful".
Her:	"And the money?"
Him:	"I thought we'd do it for the love of it".
Her:	"Of course!"
Him:	"It will win awards. It will be amazing!"
Her:	"And we'll work together?"
Him:	"Closely".
Her:	"Yeh?"
Him:	"Sure, I thought we'd take some time together by the coast, working on the script in the daytimes, exploring in the evening".
Her:	"That sounds gorgeous".
Him:	"Yeah, we can work the thing up together. I was even thinking perhaps I would take the hero's role, play opposite you. What do you think?"
Him:	"You don't have to go do you? Is that the time?"

Move to kiss: *[Turning and raising hand]* No!

He is kidnapped and thrown into the back of a white mini-van by the man from the station.

Post Kidnap.

She approaches camera: Now that, is what you call a plot point. That's how we do things round here when the story goes awry and we don't believe in what we see, the Benshi takes a hand. We step in and change the story. We take his smug smile and erase it. There is no reason for us to accept the story we are given, Ladies and Gentlemen. The author is dead and the re-edit is always possible to a man of imagination and commitment, someone with true insight and passion, someone who doesn't settle for the mindless banalities of boy meets girl, girl meets boy. Don't worry ladies and gentlemen, we can get this film back on track and make it an altogether more exciting proposition. He is taken to a dungeon somewhere and tortured, we get the make up artists in for some really graphic work, we go Ninja, we go Manga, we go Ninja, Manga, we go Ninja – Manga - Tamagotchi Tetsuo - Samurai – Hari Kari - Kawaskai, Kamikaze on his Sony ass...

[During this monologue an elderly Japanese woman appears from behind the screen walking slowly towards the Benshi. The film dissolves to black.]

Takako:	*[In Japanese until noted]* So it's you.
Benshi:	Hello?
Takako:	It's you who has been screwing up our film!
Benshi:	Hold on I'm in the middle…
Takako:	You should butt out Benshi. The audience doesn't need you. You should piss off.
Benshi:	Excuse me Madam, I'm in the middle of…
Takako:	I am Mana Fuji, the actor from the film you're screwing up. You should stop it. We don't need you, these people don't need you. You're out of date, you're an irrelevance!
Benshi:	Do we have some security?

Takako: You're not so brave now. You're a voyeur. You look, you don't do!

Benshi: I don't know what your problem is but...

Takako: I am from the film that you are ruining. You have been staring at me all these years but you don't recognise me. You are an idiot.
[In slow, deliberate English] My name is Mana Fuji.

Benshi: Mana Fuji? You? That's ridiculous... you... you look nothing like Mana Fuji!

Takako: Long time. People change. This is a film. I am Mana Fuji. You are... idiot!

Benshi: Idiot?

Takako: Idiot.

Benshi: Listen, I don't know who you are or where you're from...

Takako: I am from the film. I am Mana Fuji. You love me.

Benshi: I... I don't think I do!

Takako: Good. I'm pleased. You are... creep!

Benshi: Creep? *[To audience]* I'm sorry about this.
Listen, I'm delighted that you're Mana Fuji, from the film, and have chosen to be with us this evening for this screening. It is a wonderful film, your finest.

Takako: This is not a wonderful film. It isn't my film. I don't like it.

Benshi: Nevertheless, the audience have been enjoying it and are, no doubt, very anxious to learn how it ends, so if you could...

Takako: *[In Japanese]* I am not going to sit in the audience while you misrepresent me and the film. You should sit in the audience and watch the film. I know more about the film than you. I was in the film. You don't even speak Japanese, you have no idea what I'm saying now even! You should sit. If anyone is going to be the Benshi it should be me.

Benshi: Ladies and Gentlemen I'm afraid we are going to have to have an unscheduled intermission whilst we... *[She knocks him unconscious]*.

Takako: *[In English]* I am sorry. This man he is idiot. He makes the film bad. There is no kidnapping in this film. No

47

> *[Mimes the struggle]*. Let me show you how the film ends.

Father emerges and reads post card: Dear Father, I have met Nami, we are having a lovely time in Tokyo. I have saved up the money to come home and I will do so soon. I hope the catches have been good.

Walk in the park: I do not like the film 'Shadows'. The kiss at the end. This walk in the park. No, if this was my film I would have a different end. Now I am the Benshi I can show you a new end. You watch my film now.

Film rewind montage:
The white mini-van from the kidnap scene reverses onto scrubland. The Benshi's unconscious body is pulled from of the back by two people wearing white gloves. As these people climb back into the van they are seen to be the film's two young heros. The van leaves and the Benshi stands up, he is in the film now:

> This is my ending. The voyeur becomes the watched. Subjects become the protagonists. The Benshi is in the frame, as he always wanted to be.

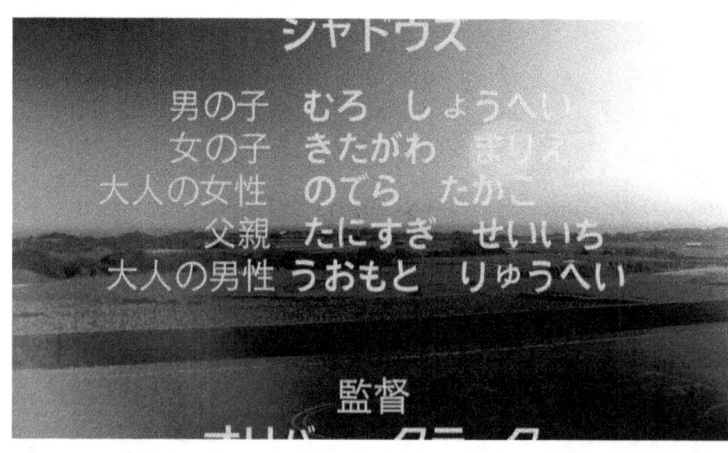

The van pulls up to a junction. The young woman is driving. In the passenger seat sits the young man. She offers him a lift back to his village. He suggests they go back to Tokyo to pick up her stuff. She declines, she won't be staying. We hear this discussion in Japanese. The van pulls off towards the village:

> We end things properly, with the fisherman thrown back into the sea and the woman, not happy ever after, but with as much chance to write her own story as anyone else.

[Takako departs and the film credits run]

Shadows (film)
Boy – Shohei Muro
Girl – Marie Kitagawa
Father – Seiichi Tanisugi
Man – Ryuhe Uomoto
Fantasy Voice – Nozomi Ogishima

Camera and Edit – Oliver Clark
Soundtrack – Nina West
Screenplay – Craig Stephens and James Yarker
Assistant to the Director – James Yarker
Director – Oliver Clark
Producer in Japan – Satoshi Fukuoka
Translator and Assistant Producer in Japan – Lisa Fukouka
Producers in England – Charlotte Martin & James Yarker
Benshi Costume – Kay Wilton
Opening Credits – Seiichi Tanisugi

With thanks to:
Minako Eshi and Satagaya Public Theatre, Tokyo.
Miura Film Commission and City, Keikyu Corporation.
Hogetsu Hotel, Ishii Taxi, Mitsuya Liquor, Hideyo Tsuda and Kakumoto Atsushi.

Original Programme Note

I learnt about the curious figure of the Benshi from an old book about the history of Japanese film. The Benshi intrigued me. I liked thinking about an audience so new to film they needed its grammar explained. I revelled in the idea that a Benshi could be the star attraction and could twist the narrative of any film they narrated. I empathised with the Benshi's fate, swept away by the march of technology and the coming of 'the talkies'.

In preparation for making this show we thought we should watch some old Japanese films and try being Benshi to them. *A Woman of Tokyo* by Yasujiro Ozu was my favourite and reading about the extraordinary lives of the two female leads was tremendously inspiring.

If there is such a thing as a 'typical' Stan's Cafe show, then I suspect this is not it, but we are excited by it and hope you like it.

James Yarker

Theatre Credits

Benshi – Craig Stephens
Mana Fuji – Takako Nodera*
Script – Craig Stephens and James Yarker
Direction – James Yarker
Lighting Design – Ben Pacey
Sound Design – Nina West
Costume – Kay Wilton

Graphic Design – Simon Ford
General Manger (Pre-Production) – Charlotte Martin
Administrator – Rowena Wilding
Executive Producer (Post-Production) – Roisin Caffrey

With thanks to:
Michelle Worthington, Nick Sweeting
David Edmunds and DEP Arts
Matt Burman, Alan Rivett and Warwick Arts Centre
Jack Trow
Ian Francis and Flatpack
Dr. Mark Crossley & Dr. Rachel King
Birmingham Repertory Theatre

Financial Support from:
The Great Britain Sasakawa Foundation and
Arts Council England

Commissioned by: Warwick Arts Centre

* In order to keep Takako's arrival on stage a surprise she was always listed in the film credits not the theatre credits.

Outline for the film Shadows

Scene 1:
WOMAN is busy and leaving for work. She is dressed smartly. She has a coat and shoulder bag (fashion not business). She wears high heals.

She is comfortable in Tokyo, comfortable with technology, busy but not stressed, today is a day she has been looking forward to – she is going to meet her old friend from her home village who she hasn't seen for ten years (since they were about 11 years old).

She has been sending him post cards occasionally. He sends her shells from the sea. She is on the subway when she opens the most recent shell. It has a little message written on it in his handwriting "see you soon".

Scene 2:
MAN is young and strong, he lives a clean simple life, fishing with his father. He is like a character out of a timeless story. For him life is uncomplicated, so he thinks that he will be able to go to Tokyo, meet his childhood sweetheart, ask her to marry him, she will say "yes" and they will return blissfully to the sea.

FATHER: He is father to the main male character. He is a fisherman who lives with just his son in an old shack by the sea. He has always lived by the sea and is content to do so. He is sad that others are not content with this life. So many people have moved away. A quiet sadness descends on him when he learns his son is to visit Tokyo.

MAN and his FATHER have been fishing all night and just returned to land. They have caught nothing, but this is not a disaster. Walking home they stop to sit by the sea and eat breakfast together. They talk about MAN's trip to Tokyo. Their language is very simple but not mundane. Their inner strength and stillness gives their simple words great resonance (although this is a silent film the actors should still learn these lines and be prepared to say them in the performance – later we will decide how much of this to turn into text to be seen on the screen).

M: Nothing today.
F: No, maybe you will have more luck in Tokyo.
M: I hope so
F: You will find her?
M: She will be waiting for me.
F: She would be a fine catch.
M: The best.
F: I don't want you to go.
M: Father, I must.
F: I will miss you.
M: I will return, I will return with her, I will be gone just one day.
F: Tokyo will swallow you, you will drown.
M: I can swim. I belong here Father, I will return.
F: And if she doesn't wish to return with you?
M: She will, she will.

We see MAN putting on his best clothes to go to Tokyo – the big city. He's never been to Tokyo before. His best clothes are not very smart but they are the best he has – maybe it is the suit he wore for his mother's funeral a few years before, since then he has grown and so the suit does not fit – he would not be comfortable in it even if it did.

MAN takes from a small pot all the money he has saved for this trip. His wall is covered in postcards sent by WOMAN from Tokyo over the years. He has a calendar on which he has been crossing off all the days leading up to today. He takes one of the postcards down and puts it in his pocket.

FATHER and MAN embrace. Then the man walks off. FATHER has a tear in his eye.

Scene 3:
At the station MAN is confused by the technology and pleased to find he can buy a ticket from a person. He does not

have enough money for the return fare, he is asked if he wants a one-way ticket. He says "yes".
On the train he writes in a small notebook – poems perhaps?

Scene 4:
WOMAN is at work, late, in an open plan office on her own. The atmosphere becomes like a horror film, she thinks she has finished when, from nowhere, more work appears on her desk, the phone rings just as she reaches the door, but no one is at the other end. She becomes desperate to escape the office, somehow the office does not want to let her go.

Scene 5
Arriving at a station in Tokyo MAN expects to be met by WOMAN. The crowded platform empties and she is not there. He finds a bench and sits to wait patiently for her. He sits still in the rush of people.

Scene 6
WOMAN is full of energy, late to meet MAN and desperate to get across town. Her taxi mysteriously breaks down in the traffic.

W: What's happening, why have you stopped? We're not there!
TD: I'm sorry I've run out of petrol.
W: What, what kind of taxi are you? Taxi's don't run out of petrol!
TD: I'm very sorry, this one has. That will be 1000¥.
W: You're joking, you don't get me where I need to go, you dump me in the middle of this traffic and you say 1000¥, you're crazy. You get nothing from me!

She jumps out of the cab and runs instead, it will be faster. She takes off her high-heeled shoes, they are slowing her down. She is from the countryside, she can run without shoes.

Scene 7
MAN would wait forever, confident that WOMAN will arrive

but he gets up to check the time on the station clock and when he gets back to the bench his suitcase has gone. He looks around and rather than finding help SECURITY GUARD evicts him from the station.

SECURITY GUARD is also KIDNAPPER. He is a strange man. He is not a real security guard. He does not belong in this world but he seems powerful. He has been sent from outside the film to make things difficult for MAN and stop MAN and WOMAN kissing.

SG: You need to leave Sir, your life is in danger.
M: You don't understand, my bag has been stolen.
SG: You need to leave.
M: I am waiting for my friend.
SG: We cannot have vagrants at the station.
M: I'm not a vagrant! I have money.
SG: Where are you staying tonight?
M: I don't know somewhere in *[choose somewhere]*, I have the address wait, it was in my case!
SG: Outside sir. I don't want to see you again.

WOMAN arrives in the station.

SG: Do you have the time?

WOMAN stops and looks at her wrist, her watch has gone. She points up to the clock.

She has missed MAN. She slumps exhausted and upset on the bench, she looks down and finds the postcard she sent to him saying where and when they would meet. He was here and now he isn't. How will she ever find him?

Scene 8
MAN is out in the city, alone. This is a new challenge. He cannot see the stars. How will he navigate? He buys food. He sets off. He leaves the last of his money at a shrine. He disappears into the city.

Scene 9
WOMAN is in her flat, casually dressed. She washes her feet. She is waiting to see if he will find her flat. She is worried for him. She looks out at the city for him. She knows he is there somewhere.

Scene 10
MAN is now starting to get a bit scared, the city is SO big and SO strange, SO difficult to navigate. Just when he is close to despair he finds a river flowing behind the tall buildings in a concrete channel. He is comforted and starts to follow the flow down stream.

Scene 11
WOMAN wakes with the TV still on. When she goes to switch the TV off she notices the shells MAN has sent her through the years. Suddenly she is inspired, she knows where to find him. She puts on her running shoes and rushes from her flat.

Scene 12
It is the fish market. Full of strange fish, WOMAN is uncomfortable in this strange world. She meets MAN. He is working there sweeping up. They are a bit shy of each other at first.

M: Can I help you?
W: Yes, I'm looking for someone.
M: I think you've found them.
W: Yes. What happened to you?
M: What happened to you?
W: Things got strange.
M; I know what you mean?
W: Do you want breakfast?
M; I've got no money.
W: Don't worry, I'll pay.
M: Thank you.
W: Will they miss you?
M: No, I'm due a break, come on!

At a street cafe they talk and laugh. They are getting to know each other again after all those years.

Scene 13
They walk on together, closer than before. They stop together. They turn together. They are going to kiss BUT! From no where MAN is dragged off by SECURITY GUARD and his HELPER. MAN is thrown in the back of a mini van and driven off.

WOMAN has been watching the kidnapping, it is so strange she does nothing to stop it. She turns to the camera, she knows this is not in the script!

Scene 14
The mini van pulls up by a ditch. The back doors are opened. But inside isn't MAN it is BENSHI. MAN and WOMAN dump BENSHI in a ditch and get back into the mini van.

Scene 15
The film has two endings. In one the MAN and WOMAN kiss as they were due to in scene 13 and FATHER reads a postcard from Tokyo.

In the second ending WOMAN is behind the wheel of the mini van MAN is in the passenger seat.

W: So where do you want to go?
    I'll take you back to the village.
M: That would be amazing, are you sure?
W: It would be nice to see the old place again.
M: Do you want to pick up your stuff?
W: No, I'm fine.
M: Is it a long drive?
W: No, I like driving, I don't do it very much.
M: You could stay, my father wouldn't mind.
W: Maybe, we'll see.

Woman Of Tokyo (1933) by Yasujirō Ozu – Benshi Script
Performed by Jack Trow at Flatpack Festival

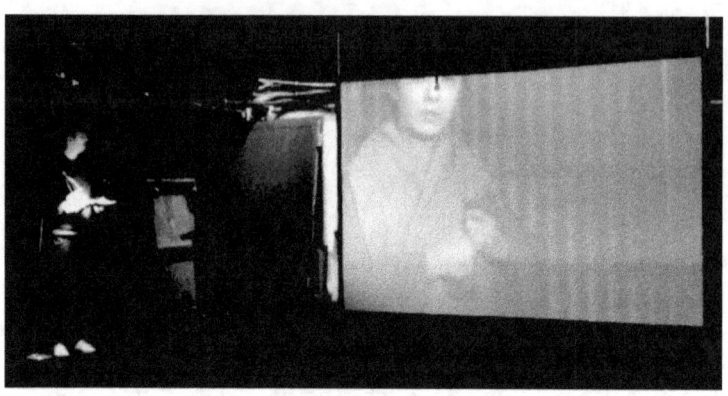

First Big Credit: This is a Japanese film.
First vertical credit: They read from top to bottom right to left.
 Many people were involved in making this film.
 There are always many people involved in making films, even small films, cheap films.
 But there is only one Benshi. I am the Benshi. I explain all films, big and small.
Opening Shot: We are inside a house.
Steamer: There is kitchen equipment.
Cutlery: People have eaten.
Ryoichi in uniform: That man is the hero. We often see the hero at the start of a film.
After text: This is not his wife. she is not his girlfriend even. She is his sister.
Socks spinning: They live together and are happy. She cares for him. Japanese socks are different to ours. In Japanese homes they do not have chairs.
 He is grateful. It is a happy day.
 She is going to have a baby. I think.
 If you look at her hand on her belly she is pregnant, maybe. Maybe it's her clothes.
 Though from this shot maybe not.
Yoshiko gives money: She is giving him money.

And some extra.
He is grateful.

Goes for coat: He is going to work, but he has no job. He is a student. He wears the uniform of a student.
The money is to pay his fees

Ryoichi leaves: They are in love because they are brother and sister.

Ryoichi returns: He does not wear make up, but the actor does.

Yoshiko apron off: She wears a beautiful kimono

Yoshiko powder on: She wears make up, the actor does as well. They are both beautiful.
She has a beautiful life.

Card: This is a new scene in a different place.

Boy leave: That boy's parents were very proud
The man in the office with the sword is a police officer. He is an officer but it is not his office.

Manager arrives: This is the manager. It is his office.
The police officer has asked the manager a question.
It is about someone who works in the office. Who could it be?

Long shot of office: One of these people.

Yoshiko: Of course, it is the woman, the sister.

Card: "That's her"

Manager & police: They are suspicious.

Yoshiko types: She is a typist.

Office: There will be questions. There will be details. "We will need evidence". "Please take a seat".

Manager with book: These are the employment records.
Ladies and Gentlemen, note how the officer compares notes from his book with the record in front of him. He is investigating.
"She has been at the company just over four years"
"Hi" (Hi is Japanese for "yes") It doesn't mean 'Hello'. Konnichiwa is 'hello'.

Manager smiles: She is a hard worker.

Manger speaks: She is generous to her brother and well liked by her colleagues.

Card: That's what I just said...
Manager: ...each day after work she visits a university professor...
Police office: ...and helps with translations.
Card: That's roughly what I said.
Officer reopens book: Now he's interested!
Card: What's this professor's name?
Talking: I don't know what's happening there.
Bowing etc: Thank you, thank you, no thank you, no thank you. The Japanese are even more polite than the English. Sorry about that.
Yoshiko: So, what is she suspected of? Could someone beautiful be guilty of something ugly?
Fingers type: She types... fast.
Credits: Well, Ladies and Gentlemen, that was an unsatisfactory film and short! I do apologise, Uzo's films are usually more satisfying than this.
Ryoichi & Harue: Ah, my mistake the brother is watching this film with his girlfriend.
The film: It's a western. No, not a western, a thriller. We are in the film. This is a famous actor.
Ryoichi & Harue: The woman has lost her hearing aid. She can't hear anything. He gives her the programme so she can work out the story. "Arigato" (that is Japanese for 'thank you'). He tries to be supportive, but he needs to watch the film.
This film is of his life. This man is him. He sees himself in this man. He completely empathises with him. He wants to commit a murder, a suicide a terrible act. This is a different man. We do not know who he is yet. He has strange socks too
Harue at door: This is the brother's girlfriend again. She lives here. Surely this cannot be her husband?
Card: Ah, she is this man's little sister.
Kinoshita: He wonders if her boyfriend's sister is home yet...
Lint picked off: I don't think this moment was in the screenplay. The actor is improvising. They liked it and kept it in.
Kinoshita gets hat: He is going out.

Harue at the door: Ladies and Gentlemen, you remember the sword and the white gloves hung up? This man is a police officer too. You see how the film gives us these clues. Always watch carefully, Ladies and Gentlemen
Card: He has something to discuss with the boyfriend's sister.
Harue & Card: "I could talk to her for you".
Laughing: "It would be easy".
Card & man: "It's not that easy, it's delicate".
Harue speaks: You can work that out for yourselves.
Kinoshita speaks: "There's a strange rumour about her at work"
Kinoshita speaks: "It seems she has been behaving in a questionable manner. She has been seen working in a disreputable bar and she's been lying about the professor".
Kinoshita: "Hi".
Card: "I'd like to trust her".
Harue kneels: Look at that composition Ladies and Gentlemen, a beautiful shot, sometimes you don't need to follow the story do you, Ladies and Gentlemen, the shapes, the lighting, the movement, the sculpture is enough.
"The Rumours are worse than that"
Whispering: You can work it out for yourselves, Ladies and Gentlemen.
Kinoshita smokes: Why is he smoking? His character is not evil or cruel, or cool or nervous, so why does he smoke? His smoking tells us nothing. But then we are not Japanese and he is smoking in Japanese, so why would we expect to understand what his Japanese smoking is saying? They agree she will go to talk with her boyfriend's sister, woman to woman. It will be better this way.
To Harue from smoke: Smoke and steam.
Ryoichi: The student studies.
Book: He is hungry for knowledge.
Shelf: Soon he will have too much.

Card:	"Is that you sister?"
Door:	No.
Ryoichi:	"Oh, it's you".
Harue:	"Is your sister not home yet?"
Ryoichi:	"You have come to see her not me?'
Harue:	This is awkward.
Card:	"I'll bet she's still busy at the professor's"
	[Look at audience] Uh oh!

Apple offered: Don't take the apple. Don't eat the apple! It's a trap. Do not bite, yes, that is it wait, don't be lured in. He is bad news!

Match Breaking: That's a mistake but they kept it in. In a the film that is a mistake but in life matches break.

Card:	"Should I pass on a message?"
	This is getting bad, Ladies and Gentlemen.
Ryoichi:	"Is it something you don't want to tell me?"
	Now you're getting the idea mate!
	Now he will reveal himself.
	He sulks. Poor friend and girlfriend and sister: poor woman. He wishes to make her feel bad and instead makes her feel worse. Do not fall into the trap! Oh dear, she's said it, she's going to tell him more.

Harue whispers: She's said it now.

Ryoichi speaks: It's cold on set.

Long shot with kettle: It has to be to let the kettle steam show. The kettle is boiling, but they do not notice. It is a sign of their intensity.

Card:	There is more.

Ryoichi turns: I thought she'd told him! He won't like this.

Ryoichi speaks: He doesn't.
    He really doesn't.
    He is angry with her but she is just the messenger.

Harue speaks & card: She explains the police are investigating.

Ryoichi walks off & card: "I trust my sister".

Card: He says the same thing more strongly.

Harue speaks: "I want to believe her too".

Ryoichi sits: He says he trusts his sister but what people say and what they feel do not always correspond.

Harue runs - he stands: For now he has his own way.
Ryoichi stops in L/S: He does not look like a victor.
Ryoichi goes to sit: In all these conflicts there is no real victor.
Kettle: Tears bubble over.
Taps: Water drips.
Women: These women are putting on make up, they are wearing make up, the actors are not.
Compact: Do you recognise her?
Yoshiko: We have not seen the sister swagger before. Normally she is demure. Now she has curly hair and more make up. Now she is in public I don't like her so much.
Kettle: The kettle has boiled dry.
Ryoichi at rice: The rice is cold
Door: A breeze blows...
Neighbour: ...as the neighbour says "There is a phone call".
Ryoichi ends call: The telephone is no ally, it can only tease and make things worse.
Car: This looks like a gangster's car.
This man looks like a gangster. He clearly has money.
Ryoichi: The rice is still cold.
All our lives are better without jealousy.
Card: Why didn't you go to bed?
There is a mountain. There is a sea. This is an end.
Yoshiko kneels: "Don't you worry about me. You just concentrate on your studies".
There is a mountain. There is a sea. This is an end.
Yoshiko talks & Card: She talks about trust.
Ryoichi & Card: "I did trust that's what makes me angry".
Card: "Why have you chosen this life?"
There is a mountain. There is a sea...
We knew the violence would come.
Look away Ladies and Gentlemen.
It keeps coming.
Yoshiko speaks & card: "Does hitting me make you feel better?"
Lip synch: "Does it?"
He should not feel sorry. He should not have done

65

that. To do that and feel sorry is not enough. Do not feel sorry for him Ladies and Gentlemen, remain resolute.

Feel sorry for her. I implore you viewers and do not be sorry for him. She is the protagonist not him. It is her film not his. *Woman of Tokyo*.

He walks away: Don't go after him. Do not touch him. Do not kiss him. Let him walk off. And slam the door behind him.

"You can hit me as much as you want, so long as you keep on studying!" No, no, no, don't say that! Say "Lay one finger on me and I will smash your skull in. In the night I will strangle you, smother you, poison you. I will not be hit! I will not suffer for your pride any more. I will not sell myself for you, you must learn to live without me because I will be gone. I don't need you. This is my film, my life and I am owning it for the first time. Touch me once more and I will sneak up to you in the night and strangle you".

Ryoichi runs off: That's it, piss off. Quick as you can...

Ryoichi to corridor: ...and don't come back!

Five years after playing this role Yoshiko Okada defected to the Soviet Union, in order to escape Japanese fascism. She went with her partner who was executed as a spy. She spent ten years in a prison camp. Afterwards she worked for Radio Moscow. She died 23 years ago aged 90.

Street: These shoes are why the socks are odd.

Ryoichi: He is a vampire, a zombie, a husk. Honour is an important thing in Japan and now he has none.

Yoshiko is slumped: His studies are abandoned. She has failed in her mission.

Ryoichi is sat: He has choices to make.

The wall light change: Dawn, Ladies and Gentlemen. We have seen these objects before, we know where we are.

Kinoshita speaks & card: "Don't worry yourself too much over it".

Harue looks at Kinoshita: That's easy for him to say.

Card: "One day he will understand, you'll see".

Kneeling: She has a parachute but she has already fallen too far.
Program: A memento of happy times. 'If I had a million'. The irony Ladies and Gentlemen.
Starting to dust: *[Knock knock]*
Yoshiko arrives: She is searching for her brother. He disappeared last night and never returned.
Yoshiko is leaving card: "There's something I must tell you".
2nd card: "I'm sorry I caused him so much anxiety".
Yoshiko Card: "I always knew he would find out sooner or later".
Harue Card: "I know I have no right to involve myself in the matter, but..." and the kicker, Ladies and Gentlemen "I feel terribly sorry for him".
The Boy Speaks: There is a telephone call.
    Can you guess what it will be, Ladies and Gentlemen?
Listening: The telephone is not your friend.
Receiver from ear: Time says it is your moment to change.
Back to her: Nothing will be the same again.
Single clock: Thin time.
The kettle: The kettle.
Yoshiko: The friend.
Harue: The mournful....
Yoshiko speaks: "What is it my dear?"
    Maybe she says "My heart is broken" and she replies "Your heart or mine?"
The flat: The flat is silent.
Noose shadow: The shadow of a noose on the wall.
    The vultures scribble.
    The man in the centre was cast because of his teeth.
Journalist speaks – card: "Do you know any reason why he might have committed suicide?"
Yoshiko shakes head: "iie". 'iie' is Japanese for 'No'.
Pencil tap question: "What was your relationship to him?"
Second tapping: This is intolerable Ladies and Gentlemen but fortunately...
Journalists enter: ...the other vultures decide to give up, they say "There is no scoop to be had here". They leave,

	hunting for fresh carrion.
Harue:	Kinuyo Tanaka was 24 when she played this role. She would become a film director, only the second woman in Japan to do so. She would be 105 now. She died when she was sixty seven.

Yoshiko sits down: I would like to live in this house.

Yoshiko speaks: She says how her brother misunderstood her. He died because of a misunderstanding.

His body (1st time): This is his body.

She calls her brother a weakling.

Journalist walk: The fat vultures walk, laughing.

The sign: News of a gang arrest.

They are talking about their profession. All is well in their world. We move on, we leave this story behind.

Final card: That was *Woman of Tokyo*.

Making A Translation of Shadows

The Background

The original idea for A Translation of Shadows was formed way back in the mid 90s. I'd found a book about the history of Japanese Film in a second hand bookshop, bought it and read the first couple of chapters; this was enough because early on it spoke about the Benshi.

Japanese theatre had a tradition of narrators so when the cinema arrived and no one understood its grammar, it made sense for a live narrator to explain the films to their audiences. I read how these narrators were significant characters who the audience would follow as fans and who could change the audience's interpretation of the film they were viewing.

At this time I had a particular interest in the dynamic between live action and screens on stage. Forced Entertainment had been playing with this idea a bit, The Wooster Group were getting very sophisticated with this and Stan's Cafe had just been bequeathed an impressive bit of digital editing kit by the National Lottery (back in the days where such funding had to be for 'additional' activities – we'd never made videos before). I was also working on an MPhil, titled Presence and Absence, which was investigating the theory around this area. It seemed like a good basis for a challenging new show.

Unfortunately, in 1998 enthusiasm within Arts Council England for funding a new Stan's Cafe show was at an all time low. The official excuse was that lots of people were proposing making shows like A Translation of Shadows but we suspected the truth was that our previous show, the uncompromisingly minimalist Simple Maths, must have got massacred in their show reports. Without money to make A Translation Of Shadows, we made a miniature show called It's Your Film, which became a hit.

Six or seven years later the Skirball Cultural Center in Los Angeles enquired about bringing them It's Your Film as part of a Film Noir season they were considering. It struck me that we could add value to this trip by bundling a new, film related show at minimal extra cost. Ian Francis, at Flatpack Festival in Birmingham, had alerted us to a 'neo-Benshi scene' around San Francisco, so we used this as leverage to suggest to the Skirball that we add a Benshi narration to one of those silent Japanese film by Ozu or Kurosawa which were influenced by Hollywood's Film Noir.

The LA gig never happened but its possibility had put A Translation of Shadows back on our agenda.

The Screenplay.
Once A Translation of Shadows was identified as our next studio theatre show the option of narrating an existing film became less interesting. We liked the idea of the Benshi altering a film's content more literally. The relationship between stage and screen could be much richer if we made the film as well as it Benshi 'translation'.

Keeping the show close to its Japanese origins felt important and this was made easier through having already worked in Tokyo twice, once with our show Of All The People In All The World and again running a week long workshop with local theatre makers. Initially we contemplated shooting the film in the UK and ordering establishing shots from a second unit based in Japan, but we didn't want the film to become a spoof, which it would have had to be for that idea to work. We felt that the film had to be 'straight' and that the easiest way to make it feel Japanese was to shoot it in Japan.

We recruited filmmaker Oliver Clark to make Shadows with us. Oliver had already seen lots of our work, had documented some of it. He had made original films for another collaborator of ours, Michael Wolters and had extensive experience making travel type programmes around the world for the BBC.

We told Oliver we wanted to make an hour long film and he advised on the number of scenes this could entail and the amount of narrative these could contain. He recommended the simplest possible story.

Craig and I worked on a screenplay that complied with Oliver's guidelines and in a series of meetings Oliver interrogated our screenplay; "What's happening here?", "Why does this happen?", "How does the audience know that?" etc. We had to make something that would work as a silent film and have enough space in it for the Benshi to add material. We didn't want the film to be so riveting people wouldn't watch the Benshi or so self-explanatory that the Benshi was redundant. We also had to work out how the Bensh's presence could be felt within the film and plot this in, of all the challenges in writing the screenplay this aspect was the most challenging.

A love story was the simplest story we could imagine and one that would address one of the show's interests, which was the constructed and seductive image of film stars. We wanted to critique 'the male gaze' without exploiting that gaze.

We wanted the film to feel as expansive as possible whilst keeping it as cheap as possible. Shooting some scenes outside Tokyo would make the film feel bigger. We hoped having a character come from the Japanese countryside into Tokyo would allow us to explore Tokyo as an alien world without it becoming a westerner's *Lost in Translation* cliché. The seaside felt a lot more poetic than the countryside so Boy became a fisherman not a farmer.

A further consideration in creating the screenplay was to write something it would be possible to film on a very limited budget on the other side of the world in five days. Our previous trips to Tokyo meant we had a feel for possible locations and so we wrote some of the story around these locations.

The Filming.
We left production work for the filming perilously late, this was a function of needing to sort the screenplay out and this was delayed because we were busy and were struggling to think far enough ahead. We scrambled round our Japanese contacts and pulled together the cast, three of whom had been on our workshop, the fourth was a recommendation. Our first contact as a 'fixer' didn't work out but eventually we hit gold with a husband and wife team of translator and producer/fixer. They worked fiendishly hard and sent through photos of locations. We worked on schedules right until the last minute.

Oliver and I arrived one day and held a planning meeting the next day when we also met the cast and sorted out their costumes (a mixture of their own wardrobes and second hand shops).

For some of the locations we had paid for permission to film. Though occasionally this had felt unnecessary, on reflection it did give us reassurance that we could work at our own pace and wouldn't be forced to move on. Other scenes were shot guerrilla style, without permission and looking over our shoulders. Every scene involved rapid decision-making, flexibility of thinking, negotiating skills and improvisation. Working via translation a lot of the time was challenging, not so much with the actors but with outside agencies. We finished having ticked everything off and came home.

Post Production.
Oliver made a very rough edit, essentially putting the film's storyboard together on screen in big lumps. At the same time Craig and I limbered up by each writing a Benshi narration for a different Ozu film. This introduced us to a number of ideas; how to deal with the dialogue cards used in silent films, how much you can say, how much you need to say and what is too much to say.

I researched the biographies of the two female leads from *Woman of Tokyo* and was stunned by them, how young they had been when they were in the film, how old they were when they died, how long ago they died and what they did between being in the film and dying. Reading those biographies helped solve a problem. Rather than making the film narrative richer we could layer actors' stories over characters' stories, with the Benshi's story oscillating between those two and our world in the theatre.

We took our film as a basic text to be deciphered and interpreted then layered additional narrative on top of that, reading into the film more than is there. Through an early try out of a small section of the performance to a few trusted people in a rehearsal room at Warwick Arts Centre, we learnt that the poetic side of the show was working, the voyeuristic element felt strong and that the sound world was under utilised.

This suggestion that we should consider moving the Benshi's voice into the same sound world as the film was helpful. We also worked up more poetry and continued to work the voyeuristic strand through the show.

Pre (Theatre) Production.
The lighting design brief highly circumscribed, the theatre light can only spill onto the screen in one, very special circumstance. After the show's theatrical introduction the lighting needed to become like dance lighting so the floor disappears and the Benshi appears to be floating in space.

Lighting designer Ben Pacey, added lighting cues in that supported moments when the Benshi diverts the film's narrative and these 'glitches', as we came to call them, then demanded their own sound effect. After elaborate programming all these cues were then triggered by computer as the film hit key cues.

In this web of automation Craig performs against the relentless march of a film which will not wait for him or catch up with him. He needs to not be staring at the screen but needs to time his delivery to mesh with events on that screen, using peripheral vision, rhythm and a lot of practice.

James Yarker
Blog post pre-opening night.

About the illustration and design

The illustrations for the covers of these books were undertaken by students at Birmingham City University as the final module of their first-year illustration course during the Spring/Summer of 2018. The images were developed using workshops using variations of the theatre-devising methods produced by Stan's Cafe but adapted and applied to the making of visual work. The resulting work was shown in the pop-up exhibition *The Something Of Somebody Something* at AE Harris in May 2018.

The design concept of the books was produced by final year Graphic Design student Aimee Chapman. These were then further developed for print in a collaborative process between Stan's Cafe and the University's Innovation Product Support Service (IPSS) and involved helping the company with selecting appropriate DTP software, undertaking training and selecting a suitable print on demand service.

Gareth Courage
Lecturer in Illustration
Birmingham City University